How to Keep

Tropical Aquarium Fish

How to Keep
Tropical
Aquarium
Fish

Jonathan Stuart

TODTRI

This book was designed and produced by TODTRI Book Publishers
P.O. Box 572, New York, NY 10116-0572 FAX: (212) 695-6984

e-mail: info@todtri.com

Printed and bound in Singapore

ISBN 1-57717-016-4

Visit us on the web!
www.todtri.com

Contents

Introduction

Overleaf: Aquarium with rustic slate

his book is intended as a guide for anyone who wants to keep tropical fish. It is divided into two parts. The first part will introduce the subject and describe the benefits and problems which come from fish-keeping. It will also give practical information regarding the heating, and lighting required and what plants to use, and conclude with a practical guide to setting up an actual aquarium in your own home. The second part of the book will contain an A-Z guide of suggested varieties of freshwater tropical and marine tropical fish for the first-time aquarist.

The newcomer to the particular hobby of fish-keeping will probably find the whole subject rather daunting. There are, as mentioned, numerous books on the subject, many aquarists who will be able to offer advice on particular aspects of aquarium maintenance and fish management, and many well-intentioned friends who have already had some experience of this very rewarding hobby. In many cases the enthusiasm of such friends can deter the beginner from continuing with the subject. But, as with many other subjects, the beginner should not be put off by the variety of advice from others. A careful, considered approach is always the best way to introduce yourself to the subject. If you intend to keep fish then you should be prepared

Opposite: A beautiful example of a freshwater tropical community aquarium with Pagoda rock and natural plants

Below: Emperor Angelfish

to listen to others who have had experience and read as much 'aquarium-based' literature as you can get your hands on. But make sure that your reading matter covers those areas which are practical for the beginner rather than the more advanced, demanding (and possibly more exotic) areas of fish-keeping and aquaria.

Because the subject of the home aquarium is so wide in its variety and so very complex in its management, it is wise to start from the very basics. If your wish is for a 'home-based' aquarium – an environment which is populated with either freshwater or marine tropical fish – there are certain considerations that you will have to make well before you even launch yourself in the direction of the local aquarium supplier.

Do you have the space available? Are you prepared to devote a little of your time to looking after the fish which you introduce and will you prove to be a responsible 'aquarist'?

This last point applies not only to the experienced enthusiast but particularly to the beginner. Maybe your interest has been awakened by an aquarium which is situated in a friends' house, or maybe you

Above: A Queen Angelfish swimming in all its glory

Opposite: The splendid geometric symmetry of a Malayan Angelfish

Overleaf: A reef aquarium with compatible inhabitants

Above: Rainbow Cichlid gently weaving through the foliage

have spotted that there are many publications on the market covering such an exotic, fascinating and relatively easy hobby. But whatever your initial motivation you must constantly remember that you have a responsibility to the fish which you finally decide to introduce into your aquarium. Although your role in the hobby is relatively trouble-free and is only demanding of the occasional feeding and general maintenance of the tank, never forget that the fish which you intro-duce have come from an environment which is totally different from that which you are setting up for them, however hard you try to dupli-cate their original home waters. Whereas certain freshwater tropicals have been used to unrestricted travel along rivers and lakes, you are now the controller of their new world and you should always provide for their requirements and their general well-being as best you can.

Keeping tropical and marine freshwater fish is an infinitely reward-ing pastime which will provide you with many hours of pleasure. It will demand relatively little time of effort from you in return and it will be an eye-opener into an aspect of the natural world which is far less available from any other hobby.

Opposite: American Flagfish

PART 1
Fish Keeping & Maintenance

Why Keep Fish?

Fish-keeping is a hobby that does not require you to expend any more, and often considerably less, effort than many other home-based hobbies. The amount of enjoyment that you will, in return, obtain from your efforts is often far more than you would gain from other such activities. If you really want to keep fish and you have the space available, it is perfectly possible for anyone to set up an aquarium in their own home.

Why you should actually keep fish is a question to which there could be any number of answers. Perhaps you would love to keep pets but you are not able, or allowed, to keep two-legged or four-legged pets in your accommodation. If this is the case, fish-keeping is a very suitable alternative. Tropical fish are comparatively undemanding. They do not take up any more space than is required for the actual aquarium, and they do not have to be taken out for walks. Once established in the home, the only requirements are that you look after them by feeding, checking their development and keeping an eye on the condition of the water in the tank – all straightforward tasks that will not take up too much of your time during each week.

Fish-keeping is also a very quiet and self-contained hobby, capable of being practised without much intrusion upon other members of the household, in the normal course of things. An aquarium in the home can also prove to be very relaxing and therapeutic and it is guaranteed to create a point of ever-changing interest and discussion.

Aquaria can be accommodated almost anywhere in the home. If you are keeping tropical fish you will need access to electricity in order to supply heating and lighting, but, once the tank is in position and you have space enough to maintain it, there is very little need to move it anywhere else.

Keeping fish need not involve paying out vast sums of money. There is, of course, an initial outlay for equipment, but after that the general running costs are very reasonable. If you plan correctly and choose fish that are not too challenging or demanding, the rewards of keeping fish will far outweigh the costs.

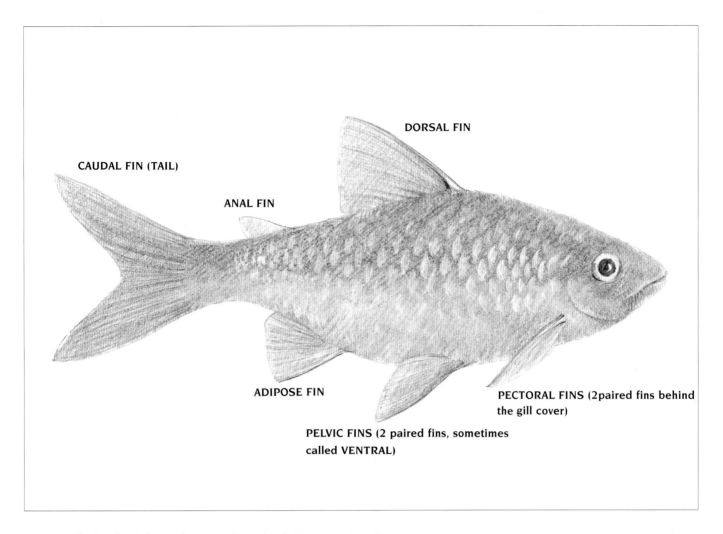

CAUDAL FIN (TAIL)

DORSAL FIN

ANAL FIN

ADIPOSE FIN

PELVIC FINS (2 paired fins, sometimes called VENTRAL)

PECTORAL FINS (2paired fins behind the gill cover)

You will also find that, after you have had the aquarium in your home for some time, you will become very curious about a great many other aspects to do with tropical fish. Where do they come from? What part of the world? Why does this particular fish have such a large dorsal fin while another one has such a strangely shaped mouth? How do they breed and what must I do to keep the fish healthy?

Keeping tropical aquarium fish is a wonderful hobby for opening up new areas of investigation and knowledge, for yourself and especially for your children. They, in turn, will learn important aspects of animal care, which should lead on to a greater appreciation of the plant and animal kingdoms. Keeping tropical aquarium fish is a fascinating, challenging and, above all, exciting pastime.

The majority of fish have three single fins (dorsal, caudal and anal) and two pairs of fins (pectoral and pelvic). A few fish also have an additional fin just forward of the tail, called the adipose fin

What is a Fish?

Whenever children are asked to draw a fish they come up with a very simple shape – an oval, slightly elongated body, a forked tail and fins. This is the "basic", universally recognized shape of a fish. There are, of course, countless variations on this basic shape, myriad combinations of colours and many subtle and often dramatic permutations on the shape of the body, the fins and the tail.

The overall shape of a fish's body and the arrangement of the fins is determined by the environment in which the fish exists and its partic-

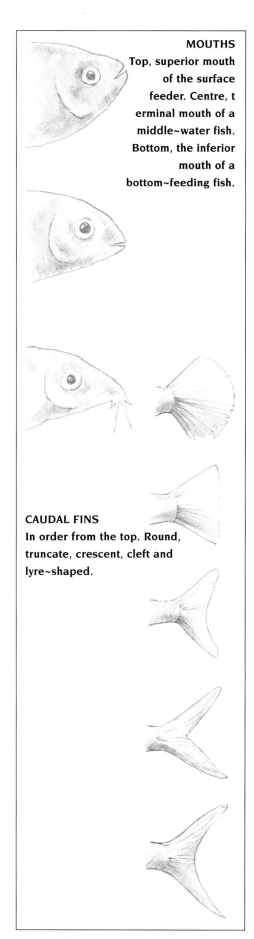

MOUTHS
Top, superior mouth of the surface feeder. Centre, terminal mouth of a middle~water fish. Bottom, the inferior mouth of a bottom~feeding fish.

CAUDAL FINS
In order from the top. Round, truncate, crescent, cleft and lyre~shaped.

ular feeding habits. For example, fish that need to swim very quickly – in fast-flowing water, for instance – have developed an elongated torpedo-shape, while the more compact, laterally compressed bodies of other fish are adapted for a less hectic environment, such as slow-moving water and often where there is are a lot of vertical reeds in the water.

The scales on a fish's body are primarily for protection, but also give a more aero-dynamic surface to the fish. All fins are used to propel the fish through the water, with the tail (caudal fin) as the main form of propulsion while the dorsal, anal, pectoral and adipose fins are used more for stability.

Fish can see, touch, taste, smell and hear. In this respect they share the same senses as we do. But fish have an additional "sense" called the lateral line system. A horizontal line of openings in the scales lies along the flank of the fish from head to tail. This arrangement enables the fish to detect vibrations and "sounds" and to identify the locations of objects or other fish.

One sure indication of the part of the aquarium in which a fish might be most at home is the position and shape of the mouth and the general shape of the body. Fish that rely on food from surface areas will have an upturned mouth and the fins on the back (the dorsal fin in particular) may not be as prominent as in other species. The bottom-dwelling fish will have a mouth that is designed to act on the surface immediately below it. These fish often have barbels (slightly extended spines around the mouth), which indicate the presence of food to them. The underside of this fish's body will be flat-bottomed. Fish with centrally placed mouths will feed mainly in middle waters, but they can inhabit almost any area of the tank seeking food.

Let us now assume that you would like to have an aquarium in your home. Your next decisions will have to be what fish will you keep? What size will the tank be? Where will it be placed in the home?

Scientific Naming of Fish

Within each family of fish there can be one or more genera, and each genus can include a number of different species.

The scientific name of a fish usually consists of two Latin words. The first word is the genus of the fish and the second refers to the species. Thus, the Festive Cichlid's genus is *Cichlasoma* and its species is *festivum*. Another member of the same family, the Firemouth Cichlid, has the same generic name but a different species title – *Cichlasoma meeki*.

The common name of each fish is the name by which it is more commonly known. However, these names can vary, whereas the scientific name is universally understood. *Cichlasoma meeki* is commonly referred to as the Firemouth Cichlid, but most reference books and journals will use the botanic name to avoid any confusion that might arise.

Breeding

The majority of aquarium fish are egg-layers. They lay their batch of eggs in specially built nests, inside caves or other retreats, directly on to rocks or plant growth, or in bubble-nests on the surface of the

water. The young of live-bearers are fertilized inside the female's body. Breeding and the after-care of both the eggs and the parents are subjects that are outside the scope of this particular book, but it is important to note the special breeding habits of the fish before you introduce them into the aquarium – some fish will consume their young if they have the chance!

A bottom~dwelling Emerald Catfish with distinctive barbels

23

Choosing the Fish to Keep

Fish that are suitable for keeping in a home aquarium can be divided into two groups – those that live in a freshwater environment and those that prefer saltwater.

Freshwater Fish

Dwarf gourami and Thick~lipped gourami in a well~established freshwater environment.

Freshwater fish are rather easier to keep than saltwater fish, mainly because the water condition required by saltwater fish is more critical. The majority of the world's freshwater aquarium fish come from the

lakes, streams and rivers of Asia, Africa and America, and can be further divided into two varieties – tropical and coldwater.

Tropical freshwater fish are far and away the most popular, and the most readily available, aquarium fish. Because these fish are so popular there are rarely any problems in finding the correct equipment or the right materials, plants and food that are required to keep these fish and, very often, no shortage of helpful and constructive advice from other owners.

Coldwater freshwater fish are far older aquarium fish, in fish-keeping terms, and were kept long before tropical fish were introduced during the last century. It is possible to keep coldwater freshwater fish in unheated tanks indoors or outdoor pools. Coldwater freshwater fish varieties are mainly represented by two well-known fish – the ubiquitous and extremely popular Goldfish and the Koi. Because of their popularity there are now many of varieties of both Goldfish and Koi, and this is a subject that is covered in far more depth in more specialized books. Koi cannot be considered ideal for the home aquarist because they grow too large for indoor tanks.

Saltwater Fish

As the title suggests, these are fish that inhabit oceans and saltwater environments, and they may be either tropical or coldwater species.

Tropical marines mainly come from the coral reef areas of the Pacific and Indian Oceans, Central America and the Caribbean. They are very popular with aquarists, not least because they include some of the most dramatically coloured and fabulously marked fish in the whole aquatic world. But – and it is a large but – they are far less hardy than freshwater tropicals and more susceptible to changes in their environment, particularly with regard to the condition of the water. They are by no means impossible to keep, even for the first-time aquarist, but it would be advisable to start off your fish-keeping career with less demanding freshwater tropicals.

Coldwater marines come from any saltwater regions away from that part of the earth referred to as the Tropics – the area between the Tropic of Capricorn in the north and the Tropic of Cancer in the south. Although keeping coldwater marines is rather less popular than tropical marines, the hobby can provide a great deal of enjoyment and can be very rewarding.

To sum up. The ideal fish for the first-timer to keep are freshwater tropicals. Having once gained experience of these, you can then move on to keep marine tropicals, which are rather more demanding and difficult to keep, but very well worth the challenge.

The Aquarium

Because fish-keeping is such a popular hobby and now that modern materials suitable for the hobby are more widely available, the range of fish tanks for the new hobbyist is very wide. In fact, almost any shape and dimension of tank is now available.

You should never, however, choose a tank purely because you think it will look attractive or dramatic in the location you have in mind for it in your home. When you buy a tank you will be taking the first step towards creating a home for your fish, a complete environment in which they will live. This "little world" should duplicate, as nearly as possible, the world from which they came, and it is essential that you cater for the particular needs of each individual fish.

The actual size of the tank is very important. There must be sufficient room in it for the fish to swim, feed and breed. If there is not enough room, the fish could, quite literally, die for lack of space. You should also bear in mind that the fish you introduce into the tank will probably grow in size. Most of the specimen fish that you see in aquatic supplier's shops are young fish, and before you buy, it is worth checking on the size the fish is expected to achieve when it is fully grown. It is far better, therefore, to get a tank that is a little too big than one that is too small. Overall conditions are easier to control in a larger tank and, once the aquarium has become established, the water chemistry will be more stable than in a smaller tank.

Surface Area

It is possible to keep fish in almost any shape of aquarium. But the surface area of the water in the tank is far more important than the overall dimensions of the tank. The standard rectangular tank, the double-cube shape, has developed over the years to provide the ideal ratio of surface area to size. In effect, the larger the surface area of the water the more efficient will be the supply of fresh oxygen to the fish and this will affect the actual the number of fish that can be housed in the tank.

What varieties of fish and how many you plan to introduce into the tank are the next areas to consider.

Opposite: Fairy Basslet on a coral reef in the Bahamas

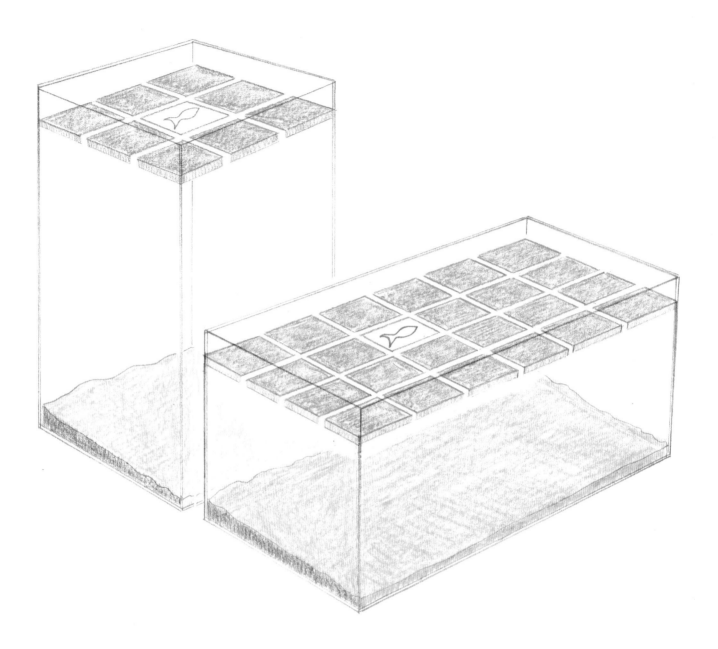

The same volume of water exists in both these tanks. But, with a smaller surface area, the taller tank can only accommodate less than half the fish of the longer, landscape tank.

Opposite: An extremely well~stocked aquarium of Festival Platy.

Some varieties fit in quite happily in a community tank and some are better suited to a tank containing only fish of the same species – a "species" tank. Once you have decided on what fish you would like to keep, it is necessary to work out how many will be comfortably accommodated in the tank. There is no hard and fast rule or magic formula that will give you a definite figure for each variety of fish. The figure also varies depending on the type of aquarium you have planned. In general, more freshwater tropical fish than marine fish can inhabit a tank of a given size, partly because marine tropicals require more oxygen than freshwater tropicals.

Perhaps the best method of calculation is to relate the relative size of the fish to the overall size of the tank in the following way. First, calculate the surface area of the tank. Then, for freshwater tropicals, allow 1in (2.5cm) of fish length (excluding the tail) for every 12sq in (75sq cm) of the water surface. For marine tropicals, allow 1in (2.5cm)

of fish length for every 48sq in (300sq cm) of the water surface.

If, therefore, you have a standard rectangular tank for freshwater tropicals measuring 24 x 12 x 12in (60 x 30 x 30cm), when it is filled with water the surface area will be 288sq in (1800sq cm). The tank can then accommodate, theoretically, twenty-two fish that are 2in (5cm) long, excluding caudal fin, or fourteen fish measuring up to 4in (10cm) in total length.

If you use the same size tank for tropical marines, you will only be able to stock about six fish measuring 6in (15cm) long. But for tropical marines it is wiser to have a larger tank than the one referred to here. A tank 36in (90cm) long is recommended.

Construction of the Tank

Fish tanks can be made of either glass – five sheets are bonded together using silicon-rubber adhesive – or acrylic plastic. The thickness of the surface glass or plastic is important because tanks carrying a large amount of water will require thicker sides.

Quite small tanks, which may be less than 20in (50cm) long, should have glass that is about 1/8in (4mm) thick. On larger tanks, over 20in (50cm) in length, this thickness would increase to 1/4in (6.5mm). Very large tanks – those over about 52in (130cm) – would require a glass thickness of 1/3in (10mm), and, because of the weight of water, some form of additional support will be necessary. It is also worth pointing out, even at this stage, that the combined weights of water and tank are far greater than one would imagine. A tank that measures 24 x 12 x 12in (60 x 30 x 30cm) will contain 12 gallons (54.5 litres) of water, which will weigh 120lb (54.5kg). To this should be added the combined weights of the gravel, rocks, plants and any other items inside the tank.

Location

Once you have decided on the size of the tank and chosen which system and what fish you would like to introduce when it is established, it is time to decide whereabouts in your home you will position the aquarium.

It is sometimes far easier to start off by working out where an aquarium should not go, rather than where it should be located. By eliminating unsuitable areas you will determine the best location.

• The tank should not be directly in front of a window, on a window sill or even in a window alcove. The dramatic increase in the temperature of a tank caused by direct sunlight can be very harmful to the controlled environment of the tank. Algal growth will also increase in tanks that receive too much light, either directly from the sun or from prolonged daylight.

• Draughts should also be avoided. So, in addition to possible draughts from the window area, do not position the tank close to the door of the room.

• Never place the tank where it might be knocked or damaged by any

moving objects. The prime example of this is that it should not be placed immediately behind a door. Any sudden noise or banging on the glass of the tank will disturb and distress the occupants.

The combined weights of water, plants, gravel and rocks must be adequately supported

● Do not place the aquarium on any item of furniture that will be unable to support the full weight of the tank. An aquarium full of water, fish, decorations, rocks and plants is very, very heavy and you must make sure that any support beneath the tank is well able to support the weight for a considerable time. Ideally, the base unit on which the aquarium rests should be custom built or be an item of furniture that you know will be strong enough.

● The tank should not be placed too far away from an electrical source. You will need to be able to connect equipment to a power

These fish are thriving because careful consideration was given to the location of the tank

source and running cables halfway around a room is not the wisest thing to do.

● Do not place the tank in front of, or over, a room radiator because this will have the effect of distorting the temperature of the water. In general, make sure that the aquarium does not get in the way of the normal everyday activity of the room.

● If, therefore, you can find a recessed area of the room, such as an alcove, this would be ideal. It would be away from the main "traffic" of the room but still prominent enough to make a dramatic display. Depending on the layout of the room, the aquarium can act as a natural room divider, particularly if it can be incorporated into a permanent structure. This has the added advantage of being seen from both sides rather than just from a straight-on viewing position.

Finally, always remember that there must be sufficient room around, and particularly above, the tank not only to allow for routine maintenance at the back and sides, but also to allow you to lift the lid in order to check the electrics, replace plants or to get at the fish.

Heat, Light & Maintenance

A tropical aquarium will require that the water be maintained at an even temperature and that there is sufficient light for the production of plant growth and the well-being of the fishes. In addition, there must be clean water and a good supply of oxygen for the fishes to be able to breathe. It should always be your aim to duplicate, as closely as possible, the habitat and environment for which the fish are best suited.

Heating the Tank

In their natural environment tropical freshwater fish exist in a water temperature of around 75°F (24°C). So, unless you choose to heat the whole of the room to that temperature, some method of heating the water and keeping it at the correct temperature is essential. Heaters are quite simple devices, the most common being the combined heater/thermostat. This consists of a glass tube containing a thermo-

Cross-section of tank showing air and water filtration

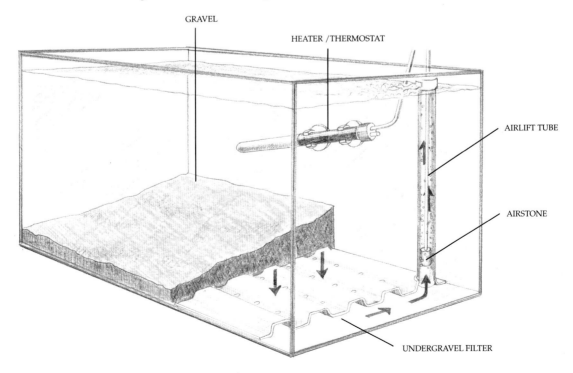

GRAVEL

HEATER /THERMOSTAT

AIRLIFT TUBE

AIRSTONE

UNDERGRAVEL FILTER

33

statically controlled heater, which operates by the basic principle that when the temperature drops below or rises above the required minimum or maximum temperature, power to the heater is switched on or off automatically. Power for the device comes via an electric cable connected to the mains. The heater/thermostat can be mounted on the side of the tank using rubber suction pads. There are also adhesive temperature strips and thermometers available, which can be fixed to the glass wall of the tank to give an instant reading.

When you are calculating the amount of heating required for your tank, a fair approximation is to allow a minimum of 10 watts of heat for every 10 gallons (45 litres) of water. When you purchase a heater for the tank, check the product literature. This should give you the necessary information for setting up and running the heater.

Lighting the Tank

The lighting of your aquarium is a far more complex subject than it might at first sight appear. We have already seen that a tank of fish should not be placed in a window because direct sunlight can raise the temperature of the tank unnecessarily, but some form of lighting will be required – and not just for the purpose of showing off your fish in the best light. However, if you leave the lights on continuously you will disrupt the life of the fish because, once again, you are trying to duplicate the natural environment which the fish is used to. You should have some portion of each 24-hour cycle when the lights are switched off. Having the lights on for about 10 hours each day is generally sufficient for both fish and plants. Lighting is also essential for the promotion of growth in plants, although the actual amount required by different plants may vary.

The amount of lighting and its duration can be controlled by using artificial lights controlled with a timing device. Both fluorescent and tungsten lights are used in most tanks. Fluorescent lighting is provided by a tube and tungsten lighting from bulbs. Tungsten bulbs generate far more heat than fluorescent strips, and this can affect, even slightly, the temperature of the tank. This will be a problem only if the water temperature in the tank is very critical. Most tanks supplied in a ready-made form will have fluorescent strips rather than tungsten bulbs.

Recommended lighting requirements for given surface areas of the tank

Surface area	Wattage
up to 350sq in (2257sq cm)	45 watts
350 - 450sq in (2257 - 2900sq cm)	60 watts
450 - 550sq in (2900 - 3547sq cm)	80 watts
550 - 750sq in (3547 - 4838sq cm)	120 watts
750 - 1000sq in (4838 - 6450sq cm)	160 watts

The above calculations are only approximate and any special requirements for your own tank should be considered.

Try not to make any sudden changes in the lighting cycle whatever cycle of lighting you finally decide upon. Fish can get very distressed if the tank is suddenly plunged into darkness. It is a very good idea to make sure that the room lights are left on for some time after you switch off the aquarium lights. This allows time for the fish to get used to the tank lights being off, just as in the natural environment the night falls over a period and not suddenly.

One very important thing to remember is that electricity and water do not mix. Lighting mounted in the hood above the tank must be protected from the water by a glass cover that rests beneath the lights and on top of the tank. All fittings within the hood must obviously be waterproof.

Good overall lighting will enhance the environment of the tank

Filtration/aeration

Water is the most important ingredient in the home aquarium, and its condition should be carefully monitored and adapted if there are seen to be any problems. The water must be clean, fresh and well oxygenated. Just adding water to a tank and leaving it to stand with no method of filtration or aeration will very soon create a stagnant environment and kill the fish. Therefore the water should be properly filtered and aerated.

A beautifully established community aquarium, with the aeration and heating equipment only just visible at the rear of the tank

Filtration

In the simplest sense, a filter is employed to ensure that the tank remains free of harmful waste and other forms of pollution. Water in the aquarium is passed through a filter and then returned to the aquarium in an improved state. There are two main ways in which this is done. Mechanical filtration deals with decayed items and with animal waste products and chemical filtration takes care of the toxic chemicals present. There are many different designs of filters on the market, the most common being the under-gravel filter and the box filter.

For the beginner the simplest form of filter is the under-gravel variety. Fixed to the bottom of the tank below any gravel or sand, water is drawn down through the gravel and the filter to be returned to the surface by means of the airlift. The more sophisticated box filter system is a device, mounted externally, which contains the various media for complete filtration. The water is siphoned into the box and then back to the tank.

Aeration

To aerate the water properly and to make sure that the water is circulated throughout the tank, thus increasing the amount of oxygen available, an air pump and an air stone must be used. The air pump runs on compressed air, which pushes air through a tube directly to the air stone. This is made of porous material and can be positioned either at the base of the airlift tube or on the surface of the substrate. Air passing through the air stone creates bubbles which rise to the surface of the water.

Below: Plecostomus resting on a gravel substrate

Plants

There are a number of reasons why plants are included in the home aquarium, apart from their obvious attractiveness in an aquatic landscape. Primarily, they are useful in the provision of oxygen into the water and for the extraction of carbon dioxide through the process of photosynthesis. For this reason it is very important that the plants receive adequate light.

Plants also help to create a landscape in which the fish can find shade from any direct light source, and they also provide an area of relative safety in which fish can spawn and lay eggs. For some fish certain plants act as an additional food source.

The greatest proportion of aquatic plants are rooted plants. Rooting plants into the aquarium is not a complicated task, as many of the modern plants come complete in their own plastic containers that can be bedded down into the gravel of the tank. Others will require a more complete form of planting, but this, too, is not a very complex task. A peat-based layer or plug can be added to the gravel substrate into which the roots can be bedded.

The present range of available plants is comfortably large and it is definitely one of the areas in which it is wise to seek the advice of the supplier and friends who already have established aquaria.

Keeping the plants healthy is also not very complicated in a well-run aquarium. The bulk of their food comes from the bacterial action on the fish faeces, but if you want to add to the supply of plant food there are specially prepared foods in both liquid or tablet form. It is, however, very important to have absolutely clean water. The leaves of the plants can become coated with any dirt in the water very easily, and this is bound to affect the plants' growth adversely.

Using Plants in the Aquarium

The simplest rule regarding where to position any of the plants is that tall plants should be placed towards the back and the sides of the tank. This will provide a "frame" for the main swimming area of the tank, and can be very useful for hiding any of the electrical connections, pumps and air-tubes that may be visible at the rear of the tank.

Opposite: A freshwater tropical aquarium containing gravel, rustic slate and very well~developed natural plants

Recommended Plants for Freshwater Tropical Aquarium

Tall or medium-tall plants that are well suited for the areas at the sides and the back of the tank include:

Bacopa monnieri (baby's tears)
Cabomba aquatica (fanwort)
Ceratophyllum demersum (hornwort)
Echinodorus berteroi (Amazon sword)
Egeria densa (waterweed)
Elodea canadensis (Canadian pondweed)
Hydrilla verticilliata (hydrilla)
Hygrophila difformis (water wisteria)
Limnophila aquatica (ambulia)
Myriophyllum aquaticum (water milfoil)
Vallisneria spiralis (vallis, eel grass)

Short or medium-sized plants that can be used for middle ground areas include:

Ludwigia repens (ludwigia)
Microsorium pteropus (Java fern)
Vesicularia dubyana (Java moss)

Floating plants that are useful for providing shade and reducing direct lighting include:

Azola coroliniana (fairy moss)
Salvinia natans (salvinia)
Riccia fluitans (riccia, crystalwort)

Bushier, lower plants can then be placed in front of this background arrangement.

If you have rocks or any other form of decoration, such as bogwood, in the foreground area, the spaces between items can be filled with short plants, which will give your landscape a more natural feel. Very low-growing varieties, spreading across the gravel base, are ideal as spawning sites for some fish varieties. Plants that float on the surface of the water are extremely beneficial for fish that are looking for shade and shelter, and they also provide a comfortable area for fry.

Bacopa monnieri

Cabomba aquatica

Ceratophyllum demersum

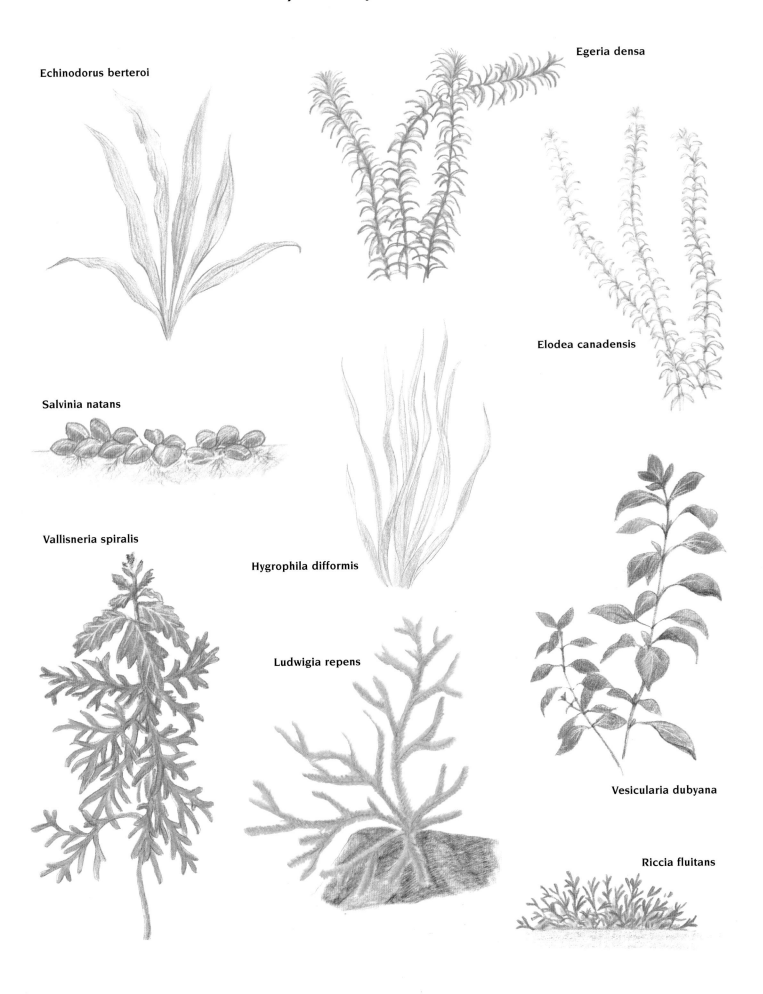

Echinodorus berteroi

Egeria densa

Elodea canadensis

Salvinia natans

Hygrophila difformis

Vallisneria spiralis

Ludwigia repens

Vesicularia dubyana

Riccia fluitans

Setting up the Aquarium

*L*ike any other household construction, the actual set-ting-up of an aquarium can be a bit of a problem and cannot be done quickly. Pre-planning is essential.

These days it is possible to buy a complete kit of parts directly from a supplier. This will contain all the necessary items for the aquarium. The alternative is to buy items individually until you have everything that you will require. Whichever method you use, the procedure for assembly will be the same.

You should have some idea of the actual landscape of the tank even before you start putting it together. Do a rough sketch showing where you intend to place the plants and any other features, such as rocks and bogwood. You can use this sketch plan when you come to start work. It need not be a great work of art, just sufficient for you to get a more exact idea of what is involved.

A carefully considered and well-established tropical reef aquarium

Before starting, you should check that you have all the items necessary for the task easily to hand. First, check that you know how you will actually put the water into the tank. It is possible, but not advisable, to fill the tank elsewhere and then transport it to the final location. It is far better to work out an arrangement for piping the water to the tank from a water source. Using buckets to transport the water to the tank can be a very messy, time-consuming and tiring exercise.

1 Make sure that you have the following items:
- The tank.
- A specially manufactured stand to take the aquarium, or suitable furniture as a base.
- The hood, complete with lights and condensation tray.
- Heater/thermostat, airline and aerator, non-return valve and diffuser stone.
- Filter and filter media.
- Gravel, stones, rocks and other items that have been planned in the landscape.
- Plants (make sure that these are kept as moist as they were when you purchased them).
- Plugs for each electrical item you will be using. (If you are using a cable-tidy, the junction box assembly from which all leads are directed, you may only need one main plug.)
- Back-up set of subsidiary equipment – algae scraper, spare fuses and so forth.

2 Make sure that the tank is completely clean and that there are no scratches on the glass.

3 Check that there are no leaks in the tank by filling the aquarium with water and checking for any signs of seepage. If there are any leaks, fix them applying a silicone-based adhesive to the areas required. (Checking for leaks need not be done *in situ*.)

4 Position the tank in the chosen site, making sure that the furniture or stand beneath is resting firmly on the floor. It is a good idea also to insert a covering of plastic or polystyrene directly beneath the tank because this will ensure that the tank is resting in a completely horizontal position.

5 Empty the tank and clean away any last minute dirt or dust marks.

6 Re-check that tank is in final position.

Filling the Aquarium

1 Place the under-gravel filter in position at the bottom of the tank and lay the gravel tidy on top (if you are using one).

2 Fit the airlift tube in position.

3 Thoroughly rinse all the gravel in water. This can best be done by

SETTING UP THE AQUARIUM

1

2

3

4

filling a bucket with gravel and allowing the water to run into it until the water runs clear.

4 Start by laying gravel on top of the filter base (which includes the gravel tidy if being used) and build up to the required depth, incorporating any rocks and any planting medium planned for the landscape.

5 Position the heater/thermostat and the airline into the airlift tube. *Note:* The heater/thermostat should be placed at a slight angle with the connection end uppermost. It should also be mounted so that it is clear of the gravel.

6 Check the temperature of the water. Very cold water can be detrimental to some plants.

7 Start to add the plants. There are three ways of doing this – putting the plants into a completely dry tank, into a tank partly filled with water or into one which is full of water. Planting the tank when it is dry means that you cannot be absolutely sure of the look of the plants until it is filled. Planting when the tank is completely full of water is more difficult than if it is only partly filled and this is the recommended method. You may be surprised by the distortion created by the water, and you might have to check several times before placing the plant in the correct position, but planting into a partly filled tank makes it easier to put plants in the final position.

8 Half fill the tank with water. Create as little disturbance to the gravel base as possible, by directing the water on to a convenient rock because this will minimize the effect on the gravel. Once you get past a certain point, any splashing effect will cease. Always run the water in at a gentle pace, even when the water rises above the hose level.

9 Continue to fill the tank, leaving a space of about 1–2in (2.5–5cm) at the top.

10 Attach and check all connections to any items you are using, such as an external filter, air pump, airlift tube, air stone and spray bars.

Fitting the Lights

1 Place the condensation tray in position on top of the tank and immediately below the hood.

2 Install the lights in the hood.

3 Check that any tubes, cables and so on do not get in the way of the hood when it is fitted.

4 Lower the hood into position and connect it to the starting gear. This item will often fit into the back of the hood.

5 Switch on and start the aquarium running.

It is now best to leave the aquarium running in this state for at least a day to check that all equipment is running properly. Check the temperature of the water, the flow of air and the condition of the water at regular intervals and adjust them if necessary.

Opinions vary about how long you need to allow for any initial running-in period. The aquarium will not be fully functioning until fish are actually introduced, but it is wise to allow a few days to iron out any problems, such as water flow, defective lighting and so on, that become evident. Only when you are absolutely sure that the environment is ready, should you start to add the occupants.

Introducing the Fish

Aquarium shops, and even local aquatic societies, are the best places to purchase your fish. Not only can you see them before buying, but you should be able to get good advice as well.

Although you will probably have a pretty good idea of the varieties of fish you are looking for before you go to the supplier, it is always worth checking on the general characteristics of the fish (such as colour, distinguishing marks and body shape) beforehand. Any fish that appears to be sluggish, does not swim easily or looks dull in general colour should be avoided. It is also not a good idea to buy fish that show any signs of possible disease.

Most of the fish on sale will be young, and, as noted, you should check on what size the fish will be when fully grown. It is equally important to find out how long the fish has been at the suppliers and if it has been quarantined.

When you have actually purchased your fish you will need to transport them home. If you are lucky the supplier will have a custom-built transport box that you can use. This will be a box that takes a plastic, water-filled container and that is lined with polystyrene to retain any

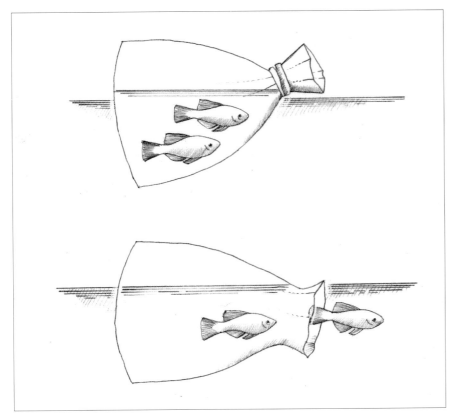

Rest the bag on the surface of the water to equalise temperature. Then untie bag and combine the tank water with that in the bag. Gently release the fish into the tank

heat. Fish should not be kept in this container for any length of time after your journey home.

Some aquarists believe that the next stage should be to quarantine the fish for a week or more, but others prefer to introduce the fish to the tank as soon as possible. Whatever method you choose, it is important to handle them with care and make absolutely sure that the tank is ready for the fish. Moving them at any time can be stressful.

The method of putting the new fish in the tank is quite straightforward. Keep the aquarium lights off. Rest the bag that contains the fish gently on the surface of the water in your tank. The aim is to equalize the temperature inside the bag with the water temperature of the tank. Leave the bag for about 15 minutes. Then untie the bag and transfer some of the water from the aquarium into the bag, and leave it in this state for a short while. Then repeat the procedure until you judge that the aquarium water and the water in the bag are the same. Then gently release the fish into the main tank.

Do not make the mistake of switching the lights on immediately after putting them in the tank to show off the new fish. Leave them to get acclimatized to their new home first. Ideally you should let them alone until the following day. They will then experience a gradual increase in daylight. Feed sparingly during that day and check that they are comfortable.

Maintenance Routines

The aquarium will not look after itself, and it will be your responsibility to make sure that the fish are healthy and that their environment is well-maintained.

Daily
1 Check the water temperature.
2 Do a head count to see if all fish are present.
3 Check visually for any signs of disease or ill-health.

Weekly
1 Top up the water level.
2 Check specific gravity (if you have a marine aquarium) and pH level using a kit.
3 Check for algal growth and clean tank walls if required.
4 Check electrical fittings.

PART 2

A–Z of Freshwater & Marine Tropical Fish

Freshwater Fish

Anabantoides

Belontia signata (Combtail Paradise Fish)

Family: Belontiidae
Length: 51/2in (130mm)
Origin: Sri Lanka

The overall colouring of the fish is golden with blue coloration in all the fins. The Combtail is distinguishable by a dark patch at the base of the rear of the dorsal fin. This species can be aggressive, and it is wise to include it only with fish of a larger size. Females are duller in colour than the male. Eggs are laid in a bubble-nest and protected by the male.

Requirements
It will take all types of food, particularly worms, insects and other live foods. Does not require any special water conditions. Temperature should be around 77°F (25°C). Good vegetation is necessary. Will use all swimming levels.

Betta splendens (Siamese Fighting Fish)
Family: Belontiidae
Length:21/2in (60mm)
Origin: Southern Asia

Because of planned breeding, aquarium varieties of the Siamese Fighting Fish have a wide range of colours and very dramatic fins. Because the male is very aggressive, it is important not to have two in the same tank together. But they are tolerant of females and other species. The male builds a bubble-nest, and the female produces up to 500 eggs. Males should be raised separately.

Requirements
Will take all foods, including live foods. Water conditions are not critical. Temperature can be between 75 and 82°F (24–28°C). Vegetation necessary. Will use all swimming levels.

Colisa chuna (Honey Gourami)
Family: Belontiidae
Length:21/2in (60mm)
Origin: India

The small, rather stocky Honey Gourami is a shy and retiring fish. It is best kept in a species tank, although it can manage in a community. Golden-brown in colour. with yellow dorsal and ventral fins. The female is less colourful. The coloration of the male becomes more pronounced at breeding time. A bubble-nest builder, which the male guards for several days.

Opposite: Belontia signata (Combtail Paradise Fish)

Below: Colisa chuna (Honey Gourami)

Below: Betta splendens (Siamese Fighting Fish)

Opposite: Colisa labiosa (Thick-lipped Gourami)

Requirements
All live foods taken, including worms and crustaceans. Water conditions are not critical. Temperature should be between 75 and 79°F (24–26°C). Good vegetation is required. Will swim in all levels.

Colisa labiosa (Thick-lipped Gourami)
Family: Belontiidae
Length:21/2in (70mm)
Origin: Southeast Asia

The thick upper lip of this Gourami gave it its popular name. The body is reddish-grey in colour with bands of silver-blue stripes. The overall colour of the male changes at breeding time to a dark chocolate. A bubble-nest builder, with the female producing over 500 eggs. It is wise to move the female after she has spawned because the male can become very aggressive.

Requirements
Will take worms, insects and other live foods. Does not require any special water conditions. Temperature 75–78°F (24–25°C). Happy with a mixed plant and rock habitat. Will utilize all swimming levels.

Helostoma temmincki (Kissing Gourami)
Family: Helostomatidae
Length:8in (200mm)
Origins:Southeast Asia

Below: Helostoma temmincki (Kissing Gourami)

The "kissing" habit of this Gourami is not a sign of affection but probably a form of sparring with other members of species. Both sexes appear very similar with a grey-green, silvery body. Older males are more colourful. Eggs are free-floating and rise to the surface or adhere to plants on the way. A pinker coloured version of this Gourami is also available.

Requirements

Will take all foods, but there must be a good supply of vegetable matter included. Will tolerate most water conditions. Temperature between 75 and 83°F (24–28°C). A fair amount of plants necessary, including some floating plants. Will swim at all levels.

Macropodus opercularis (Paradise Fish)

Family: Helostomatidae
Length:31/2in (80mm)
Origin: China, Korea, Vietnam

One of the earliest tropical fish to be introduced into Europe (in about 1870). Colourful and quite aggressive, the general coloration is with red and bluish-green bands running across the flanks. Dorsal and anal fins become redder towards the tips and in the male they are

Macropodus opercularis (Paradise Fish)

elongated. A bubble-nest builder and excellent for cleaning algal growth from the tank.

Requirements
Will take both live and dried foods. Does not require special water conditions. Can tolerate a wide temperature range, from 59 to 77°F (15–25°C). Some floating plants and dense vegetation necessary. Will use all swimming levels.

Left: Trichogaster Leeri (Pearl or Lace Gourami)

Trichogaster Leeri (Pearl or Lace Gourami)
Family: Belontiidae
Length:4l/2in (110mm)
Origin: Southern Far East

A peaceable fish, which prefers a densely planted environment. Both males and females are similar in coloration, with a silver-brown upper body and an orange tinge to the lower body. On the female the lower body is more silver-white. Both have a dark line starting at the mouth and extending past the eye and along the body. Pelvic fins are long and threadlike.

Below: Trichogaster trichopterus (Three-spot Gourami)

Requirements
Will take all foods. Comfortable in all water conditions. Temperature range 75–86°F (24–30°C). Vegetation should have areas of dense growth and some floating plants. Will use all levels for swimming.

Trichogaster trichopterus (Three-spot Gourami)
Family: Belontiidae
Length:4l/2in (110mm)
Origin: Southeast Asia

Similar in shape and size to the Pearl Gourami. The general colouring of both sexes is silver-green, and the male has larger dorsal fin. This Gourami takes its common name from the two dark spots along its flank. The third spot being made up from the eye. A peaceable fish, which builds a bubble-nest on the surface.

Requirements

All foods accepted. Water conditions not critical. Temperature range of 73–82°F (23–28°C). Good general vegetation necessary. Will use all levels for swimming.

Characins

Family: Characidae
Length: 3 1/2in (90mm)
Origins: Central America

The Blind Cave Fish has no eyes. Its natural habitat is underground waters, which are totally dark, and it navigates by the lateral line method. Fins are pale in colour and almost transparent. The body is also pale but with a silver-blue appearance. It is peaceful and can be kept in a community tank.

Requirements

Will take most foods, both live and dried. Soft or medium-hard water is suitable. Temperature between 68 and 86°F (20–30°C). Uses the middle to lower swimming areas of the tank.

Astyanax mexicanus (Blind Cave Fish)

Cheirodon axelrodi/Paracheirodon axelrodi (Cardinal Tetra)

Family: Characidae
Length: 1 1/2in (45mm)
Origins: Northern part of South America, particularly the tributaries of the Orinoco and Rio Negro

The Cardinal's most distinguishing feature is the iridescent blue horizontal band running from the mouth right through to the base of the tail. Below this line the body is bright red. The fins are colourless. Females can be slightly larger than the males. They are best kept in a shoal, not only for their dramatic effect. The female scatters the eggs.

Requirements

Will take most live and dried food. Soft to medium-hard water. Temperature range of 71–77°F (22–25°C). Prefers the middle swimming level. Fine-leaved plants and bogwood would be an advantage.

Cheirodon axelrodi/Paracheirodon axelrodi (Cardinal Tetra)

Gymnocorymbus ternetzi (Black Tetra)

Gymnocorymbus ternetzi (Black Tetra)
Family: Characidae
Length:21/2in (60mm)

Origins: South America, particularly the Matto Grosso, Rio Paraguay
An excellent fish for the beginner. This oval-bodied Tetra is dark olive green with three darker bands running vertically over the flanks. The female is just a little larger than the male. Eggs are produced and scattered throughout the tank. It is important to remove the fish from the tank if the fish begin to eat the spawn.

Requirements
Accepts all foods, both live and dried and surface live foods. Water conditions are not critical. Temperature range is 75–80°F (24–27°C). Upper and middle swimming levels used. Some vegetation required.

Hemigrammus rhodostomus (Rummy-nosed Tetra)
Family: Characidae
Length:2in (50mm)
Origin: South America, Amazon river

Called "rummy-nosed" after the bright red colouring of its nose, this Tetra is peaceful and shy with quite dramatic black and white colouring of the caudal fins. It is not, however, a particularly easy fish to keep. It is very sensitive to changes in the water condition. It lays only a few eggs and the fry are delicate.

Requirements
Takes all foods. Water should be soft to medium-hard. Temperature range 74–79°F (23–26°C). Vegetation and other features required. Uses all swimming levels. Sensitive to changes in water condition.

Hyphessobrycon pulchripinnis
(Lemon Tetra)

Above: Hemigrammus rhodostomus
(Rummy-nosed Tetra)

Family: Characidae
Length:2in (50mm)
Origin: South America, Amazon basin

The Lemon Tetra has a beautiful, delicate yellow tinge to its otherwise silvery body, and bright red marking to the top of the eyes. Females are slightly larger than the males, which have small hooks on the anal fin. The female is an egg-scatterer and may produce fewer eggs than other Tetras.

Below: Hyphessobrycon pulchripinnis
(Lemon Tetra)

Requirements

Most foods are taken, but make sure there is a supply of surface live foods. Soft to medium-hard water. Temperature about 77°F (25°C). Well-planted aquarium with plenty of vegetation. Shoaling in the middle to lower levels.

Hyphessobrycon erythrostigma (Bleeding Heart Tetra)

Family: Characidae
Length: 1 1/2in (45mm)
Origin: South America, particularly Colombia

The Bleeding Heart Tetra is so named because it has a distinctive red mark just behind the gills. The overall body colour is light brown with a darker brown towards the top, changing to orange at the belly. The dorsal fin of the male is far more prominent than on the female. These Tetras are rather difficult to breed, but they do live longer than other Tetras.

Requirements

Will take most foods but has a preference for live surface food. Water conditions are not critical. Temperature range 73–79°F (23–26°C). Well-established vegetation is essential. All swimming levels are used.

Hyphessobrycon erythrostigma (Bleeding Heart Tetra)

Moenkhausia pittieri (Diamond Tetra)

Moenkhausia pittieri (Diamond Tetra)

Family: Characidae
Length:21/2in (55mm)
Origin: Northern South America, Venezuela

Silvery-bodied but with a gold iridescence, the Diamond Tetra has a light violet-coloured back and fins. In the male the dorsal and anal fins are sometimes well developed. The female can be quite prolific and eggs are scattered.

Requirements
Accepts all foods, but this must include some plant matter. Water conditions should be soft to medium-hard. Temperature range 72–81°F (22–27°C). Will inhabit all swimming levels. Plant growth necessary, with areas clear for swimming.

Nematobrycon palmeri (Emperor Tetra)

Family: Characidae
Length:21/2in (55mm)
Origin: Northern South America, Colombia

The Emperor has quite dramatic colouring, which is seen to advantage in a dark, well-vegetated tank. The body is olive green with dark colouring below the centre line and an iridescent bluish line between the head and the caudal fin. The eye is a brilliant blue and, in the

Nematobrycon palmeri (Emperor Tetra)

male, the dorsal fin is sickle-shaped and the caudal fin longer than the female. An egg-scatterer.

Requirements

Will take both live and dried foods. Soft to medium-hard water required. Temperature should be around 75°F (24°C). Uses all swimming levels. Will need floating plants in the tank.

Paracheirodon innesi (Neon Tetra)
Family: Characidae
Length: 1 1/2in (40mm)
Origin: South America, Upper Amazon

A brilliantly coloured Tetra, which was once more popular than the well-known Cardinal Tetra. The Neon has something of the same coloration, with an iridescent blue line from head to caudal fin and brilliant red on the rear portion of the lower flanks. An egg-scatterer.

Requirements

Accepts both live and dried foods with some plant matter included. Soft to medium-hard water required. Temperature should be between

70 and 79°F (21–26°C). Prefers middle to lower swimming levels. Likes seclusion so include some floating plants.

Paracheirodon innesi (Neon Tetra)

Cichlids

Apistogramma agassizi
(Agassiz's Dwarf Cichlid)
Family: Cichlidae
Length:Male 3in (75mm), female 21/2in (60mm)
Origin: South America, Upper Amazon

A light brown-golden body with a pronounced darker stripe running from head to base of the tail. The back of the fish is blue-green and the dorsal fin of the male is long and comes to a point. The colouring of the female is paler and more yellow. Eggs are laid in cavities and are often protected by the female.

Requirements
Will take all foods, but particularly live food. Soft to medium-hard

Apistogramma agassizi (Agassiz's Dwarf Cichlid)

water. Temperature range between 62 and 66°F (17–19°C). Vegetation and rocks required in the tank. Prefers shady areas. Will use all swimming levels.

Apistogramma ramirezi (Ram, Ramirez Dwarf Cichlid, Dwarf Butterfly Cichlid)

Family: Cichlidae
Length: 21/2in (70mm)
Origin: South America, Venezuela and Colombia

A rather timid and retiring Cichlid. Very colourful with a greenish-blue body, violet-coloured scales and overlaid with a couple of darker, purple patches. It has a darker line running through the eye to the base of the caudal fin. The dorsal fin is more developed in the male. Eggs are laid on a flat stone or in a depression in the gravel. Both parents guard the eggs.

Requirements
Accepts all foods, including live food. Soft water, which should be changed fairly regularly. Temperature around 79°F (26°C). Rocks and vegetation necessary. All swimming levels used.

Apistogramma ramirezi (Ram, Ramirez Dwarf Cichlid, Dwarf Butterfly Cichlid)

Aequidens pulcher (Blue Acara)
Family: Cichlidae
Length:6in (150mm)
Origin: South America, Venezuela

The main coloration is grey-green with scales of an iridescent blue. The dorsal and anal fins of the male are more developed than those of the female and have pointed ends. The large dorsal fin also has a yellow-red edging in both males and females. Eggs are laid on a rock and both parents tend the eggs and fry.

Requirements

Will accept all foods. Water condition not critical. Temperature between 64 and 77°F (18–25°C). Vegetation required. Will swim in all levels of the tank.

Astronotus ocellatus
(Oscar, Peacock-eyed Cichlid)

Family: Cichlidae
Length: 12in (300mm)
Origin: Northern South America

There are several varieties of this attractive Cichlid available. Oval in shape, it can grow rapidly, but is still very popular. They have dark brown bodies with irregular patches of yellow or orange. Fins are lighter in colour but darkening towards the outside. At the base of the caudal fin there is a distinctive orange and black spot. Eggs are laid on to a rock and guarded by both parents. Acaras may become aggressive to other fish.

(Oscar, Peacock-eyed Cichlid)

Requirements

Takes both live and dried foods. Water condition is not critical.
Temperature between 68 and 77°F (20–25°C). All swimming levels
used. Rocks, roots and floating plants necessary.

Cichlasoma festivum
(Festive Cichlid, Flag Cichlid)

Family: Cichlidae
Length:51/2in (145mm)
Origin: South America, Amazon basin

There is always a diagonal black band extending from the eye to
the rear of the dorsal fin. The other coloration of the Festive
Cichlid can vary, but is generally greenish-brown on the back and
paler lower down on the flanks. There is usually a dark blotch on the
base of the caudal fin. Eggs are laid on a leaf or rock and guarded
by both fish.

**Cichlasoma festivum (Festive Cichlid,
Flag Cichlid)**

Requirements

Will take all foods, but there should be some vegetable matter included. Water conditions are not critical but soft to medium-hard preferred. Temperature around 77°F (25°C). Tends to use the middle and lower swimming areas. Rocks and plants necessary.

Cichlasoma meeki (Firemouth Cichlid)

Family: Cichlidae
Length:Male 6in (150mm), female 41/2in (120mm)
Origin: Central America

Its popular name derives from the reddish coloration of its throat and underside. Apart from these areas the fish is generally blue-grey on the back and yellowish towards the belly. There are also a number of vertical bars of a darker colour. The caudal, dorsal and anal fins are coloured with lines of blue dots. Deposits eggs on the bottom of the tank.

Requirements

All foods are accepted both live and dried. Medium-hard water pre

Cichlasoma meeki (Firemouth Cichlid)

ferred. Temperature range 75–81°F (24–27°C). Uses middle and lower swimming levels. Rocks, plants and roots required.

Etroplus maculatus (Orange Chromide)
Family: Cichlidae
Length:31/2in (85mm)
Origin: India and Sri Lanka

The Orange Chromide can be very yellow in colouring but the body is marked with many reddish-brown dots making the fish appear more gold than yellow. The fins are not as pronounced as on other cichlids. Males and females are very similar. Eggs laid on a rock or similar surface and guarded by the parents.

Requirements
Most foods accepted, but should include some vegetable matter. Water should be hard, fresh with a slight salt content. Temperature range 71–79°F (22–26°C). Rocks and a few plants required. Will use the middle and lower swimming levels.

Etroplus maculatus (Orange Chromide)

Hemichromis bimaculatus (Jewel Cichlid)

Hemichromis bimaculatus (Jewel Cichlid)

Family: Cichlidae
Length:51/2in (130mm)
Origin: Tropical Africa, Nile, Niger, Zaire

The overall colour of the Jewel Cichlid is an iridescent greenish-blue. A dark band extends from the gill cover to the base of the caudal fin. One or two pronounced dark blotches appear on the flanks. Colours intensify during spawning. Eggs are laid on rocks or stones at the base of the tank.

Requirements

Will take all foods, particularly live. Water condition not critical. Temperature range 74–83°F (23–28°C). Plants could suffer as this Cichlid digs repeatedly. Swims in all levels.

Hemihaplochromis multicolor (Egyptian Mouth-brooder)

Hemihaplochromis multicolor (Egyptian Mouth-brooder)

Family: Cichlidae
Length: 3in (75mm)
Origin: Egypt, East Africa

Very suitable for the beginner. Multicoloured from yellow to a deep orange-red. The female is duller in colour than the male. Eggs are laid in a depression in the gravel base. After delivery the eggs are incubated in the female's mouth for about 10 days.

Requirements
All foods taken, including insects, chopped meat and dried food. Water condition not critical. Temperature range 68–79°F (20–26°C).

Plants, bogwood and rocks, with some floating plants required. Will use all levels.

Oreochromis mossambicus (Mozambique Mouthbrooder)
Family: Cichlidae
Length:121/2in (325mm)
Origin: East Africa

A large species, grey-green in colour and not recommended for a small tank. It can become aggressive and might uproot plants. It is, however, very hardy and is an interesting specimen for the home aquarium. During breeding the male changes colour and becomes very blue. Eggs are laid on rocks and both parents are attentive.

Requirements
Plant matter, live and dried food all taken. Water condition not critical. Temperature about 77°F (25°C). Some plants, rocks and bogwood should be included, but this fish will uproot plants in a small aquarium.

Oreochromis mossambicus (Mozambique Mouthbrooder)

Pelvicachromis pulcher (Kribensis)

Pelvicachromis pulcher (Kribensis)
Family: Cichlidae
Length:Males 4in (100mm), female 31/2in (80mm)
Origin: West Africa, Nigeria

The distinctive Kribensis has an elongated dorsal fin, which is rounded on the female and pointed on the male. There are spots on the caudal fin and a bright red blotch on the lower flanks of both sexes. A retiring species, which secretes its eggs in caves or roots.

Requirements
Will take all foods, meat in particular. Water content soft to medium-hard and it can be slightly salty (1 teaspoonful of salt for every 4 pints/2 litres of water). Temperature around 77°F (25°C). Rocks and roots necessary for shelter and fairly dense vegetation. Uses all swimming levels.

Pterophyllum scalare (Angelfish)
Family: Cichlidae
Length:41/2in (105mm)
Origin: South America, Amazon

One of the most easily recognized and popular of aquarium fish and available in many forms. It has distinctive long dorsal and anal fins and thread-like pelvic fins. General coloration is silver-brown with a few vertical bars of darker colour. They are excellent parents depositing eggs on plants and stems.

Requirements
Accepts all foods, particularly live food. Water condition is not critical,

Pterophyllum scalare (Angelfish)

but soft to medium-hard is preferable. Temperature range (73–80°F (23–27°C). Well-vegetated tank with some rocks required. All levels used.

Symphysodon discus (Discus, Pompadour Fish)
Family: Cichlidae
Length:6in (150mm)
Origin: South America, Amazon and Rio Negro rivers

An almost circular-bodied Cichlid, which is brownish in colour with vertical bars of darker colour. There are also iridescent blue patches running from the body onto the dorsal fin. Although this fish is very attractive to aquarists it is not recommended for the beginner. It requires very specific conditions and can suffer easily.

Requirements
Will take live foods and some plant matter. Water conditions are critical. Soft, acid water is essential. Temperature should not be below

77°F (25°C), preferably between 80 and 86°F (27–30°C). Well-planted tank with rocks and roots. Will use all swimming levels.

Cyprinids

Barbus conchonius (Rosy Barb)

Family: Cyprinidae
Length: 4in (100mm)
Origin: Northeastern India

An excellent fish for the beginner. It is hardy, colourful and breeds easily. The rosy-metallic colours darken to red during breeding. The fins of the female are duller than the male's. An egg-scatterer, but take care that the fish do not eat the eggs by removing them from the tank.

Requirements

Will take all types of food, particularly live foods. Water conditions not critical but should be soft to medium-hard. Temperature about 75°F (24°C). Plants and rocks required. Uses middle to lower swimming levels.

Barbus nigrofasciatus (Purple-headed Barb, Black Barb, Ruby Barb)

Barbus nigrofasciatus (Purple-headed Barb, Black Barb, Ruby Barb)

Family: Cyprinidae
Length:21/2in (55mm)
Origin: Sri Lanka

Suitable for the beginner. General coloration is more golden than that of the Rosy Barb and with distinct red colouring to the heads of both sexes. The body darkens considerably during breeding. Male fins are darker than the female's, with the dorsal being very dense.
This Barb is an egg-scatterer.

Requirements

Accepts both live and dried foods. Water conditions not critical, soft to medium-hard, and avoid raw water. Temperature about 75°F (24°C). Well-planted, but allow for good swimming spaces. All swimming levels used.

74

Barbus schwanenfeldi (Tinfoil Barb)
Family: Cyprinidae
Length: 13 1/2in (350mm)
Origin: Southeast Asia

Barbus schwanenfeldi (Tinfoil Barb)

A silvery coloured Barb, with red or orange coloration on the fins.
It can grow quite large, but smaller specimens are suitable for the
aquarium. It is also very partial to tank vegetation. It is active and
can jump well, so a lid on the tank is essential. The female
scatters her eggs.

Requirements
Will take all foods, both live and dried foods. Plant foods should defi-
nitely be included as this fish eats pool vegetation. Water should be
soft to medium-hard. Avoid raw water. Temperature about 75°F (24°C).
Allow good swimming spaces with plants restricted to back and sides.
Uses all swimming levels.

Barbus schuberti
(Schubert's Barb, Golden Barb)

Family: Cyprinidae
Length: 2 1/2in (65mm)
Origin: Various opinions regarding whether this barb comes from
Southern Asia or is "man-made" from cross-breeding other barb forms

Although the exact origin of the fish is unknown it is a hardy and
attractive aquarium fish. Golden-yellow with slightly paler coloration
on the belly. Dark patches can be seen just below the dorsal fin and at
the base of the caudal fin. Females are slightly plumper and very prolific.

Requirements

Will take all dried and live foods. Water condition is not critical.
Temperature range 68–77°F (20–25°C). Well-planted tank required.
Swims in the middle to lower levels.

**Barbus schuberti (Schubert's Barb,
Golden Barb)**

Barbus tetrazona
(Tiger Barb, Sumatra Barb)

Family: Cyprinidae
Length: 2 1/2in (55mm)
Origin: Sumatra and Borneo

Suitable for the beginner, the Tiger Barb takes its name from the vertical dark stripes, which cross the silvery body. The anal and dorsal fins have a distinctive red outer edging. Males also have a reddish nose. They may occasionally nip the fins of other fish in the tank.

Requirements
Accepts most foods. Water should be soft to medium-hard. Temperature between 70–84°F (21–29°C). Vegetation to be kept to the back and sides of tank to allow swimming spaces. Middle and lower levels used for swimming.

Barbus tetrazona Tiger Barb, Sumatra Barb)

Brachydanio albolineatus (Pearl Danio)

Brachydanio albolineatus (Pearl Danio)
Family: Cyprinidae
Length:21/2in (60mm)
Origin: Southeast Asia

A slim fish with a forked caudal fin. The overall colouring is silver-blue with gold lines along the flanks. The female is slightly plumper and duller in colouring. Peaceful and a lover of sunlight. The female can lay over 500 eggs, and it is wise to protect the eggs from the parents.

Requirements
Will accept most foods. Water can be soft to medium-hard. Temperature range is 70–77°F (21–25°C). Well-planted tank required. Swims in the upper and middle levels. *Note*: Very active in the upper levels so a lid is essential.

Brachydanio frankei (Leopard Danio)
Family: Cyprinidae
Length:21/2in (55mm)
Origin: Southeast Asia (There is some doubt about its definite origins. Some maintain that it is a breed of the Zebra Danio (B. *rerio*). Opinions differ.)

A fast-swimming Danio, with leopard-like spots on a light golden body. The female is slightly larger than the male. As with the Tiger Danio, eggs should be protected from the parents.

Brachydanio frankei (Leopard Danio)

Requirements

Will take most foods, either live or dried. Water condition not critical but should be soft to medium-hard. Temperature around 75°F (24°C). Plants required, but make swimming areas available. Upper and middle levels used for swimming.

Brachydanio rerio (Zebra Danio)

Brachydanio rerio (Zebra Danio)
Family: Cyprinidae
Length: 1 1/2in (45mm)
Origin: Northeastern India

The body of the Zebra Danio is made up of alternating horizontal stripes of deep blue and either white or gold which extend over the caudal fin. In addition the anal fin is also patterned in the same direction. The male is more colourful, but slightly smaller, than the female. Hardy and very suitable for the beginner. Eggs must be protected from the voracious parents.

Requirements
Accepts most foods, both dried and live. Water should be soft to medium-hard, but avoid raw water. Temperature about 75°F (24°C). Leave space for swimming in a well-planted tank. Swims in the upper and middle levels.

Epalzeorhynchus kallopterus (Flying Fox)
Family: Cyprinidae
Length: 5 1/2in (140mm)
Origins: Borneo and Sumatra
A Barb with a more elongated body than other members of the genus. Distinguished by barbels and two horizontal stripes running the length of the body. The upper band is yellow, and immediately below is a black band. The main colour of the body is brown at the top and white at the bottom. Breeding methods are unknown

Requirements
Will accept most foods, but vegetable matter important. Water condition should be soft to medium-hard. Temperature about 75°F (24°C).

Dense vegetation and some rocks required. Middle and lower swimming levels used.

Epalzeorhynchus kallopterus (Flying Fox)

Tanichthys albonubes (White Cloud Mountain Minnow)

Family: Cyprinidae
Length: 1 1/2in (45mm)
Origin: China

The overall colouring is iridescent dark brown on the back and white on the belly. It also has a gold band along the flanks, bordered with blue bands. The White Cloud Mountain is a very hardy species and is very tolerant of lower temperatures. It is, therefore, a good beginner's fish. It is an egg-scatterer, but eggs should be protected.

Requirements
Both live and dried foods are taken. Water should be soft to medium-hard. Temperature can be between 62°F (17°C) in winter and 75°F (24°C) in summer. Some plants required as this fish is used to mountain streams. Middle and upper swimming levels used.

Rasbora heteromorpha
(Harlequin Fish, Red Rasbora)

Family: Cyprinidae
Length: 1 1/2 in (40mm)
Origin: Southeastern Asia, Malaya, Thailand

Rasbora heteromorpha (Harlequin Fish, Red Rasbora)

The Harlequin has been a favourite with aquarists from the early part of this century. General coloration is silver, with a pinkish hue to the

flanks and violet on the back. Its most distinctive feature is a triangular blue-black patch reaching from the middle of the body and diminishing towards the tail. Females scatter their eggs among the vegetation.

Requirements
Will take most live and dried foods. Soft to medium-hard water required. Temperature range 72–77°F (22–25°C). Vegetation should be dense with areas for swimming. Uses all levels for swimming.

Rasbora trilineata
(Scissortail, Three-line Rasbora)
Family: Cyprinidae
Length:5 1/2in (130mm)
Origin: Southeastern Asia, Malaya, Sumatra, Borneo

The Scissortail appears, in some lights, to be translucent as the general colouring is pale olive green to silver. It has a deeply forked tail with

Rasbora trilineata

(Scissortail, Three-line Rasbora)

a pronounced dark patch on each section. When resting the Scissortail twitches its tail constantly. The female is an egg-scatterer, and the eggs must be protected from the parents.

Requirements

Live and dried foods accepted, surface live foods preferred. Water should be soft to medium-hard. Temperature 70–77°F (21–25°C). Areas of open water are necessary for swimming, but keep plants to back and sides of tank. Prefers upper levels for swimming.

Other Egg-layers

Catfish

Brochis splendens (Short-bodied Catfish, Emerald Catfish)

Family: Callichthyidae
Length: 3in (75mm)
Origin: South America, Brazil, Ecuador

Brochis splendens (Short-bodied Catfish, Emerald Catfish)

The Short-bodied Catfish is often confused with the Bronze Corydoras, but the dorsal fin of this variety has a far longer base and the head is more pointed. General coloration is olive green with a metallic sheen. Eggs are deposited on vegetation.

Requirements
Will accept most live or dried foods. Water condition is not critical. Temperature about 77°F (25°C). Tank can be well planted. Uses the lower swimming level.

Corydoras aeneus
(Bronze Corydoras, Bronze Catfish)
Family: Callichthyidae
Length:21/2in (70mm)
Origin: Northern South America

Similar in appearance to the Short-bodied Catfish, but with a shorter base to the dorsal fin and a general coloration as its common name implies. It scavenges for waste food and this is just one reason for its popularity. Eggs are deposited on plants.

Corydoras aeneus (Bronze Corydoras, Bronze Catfish)

Corydoras julii (Leopard Catfish, Leopard Corydoras)

Requirements

Will accept most dried or live foods. Water conditions are not critical but not too acid. Temperature 64–77°F (18–25°C). Only a few plants necessary, with pebbles on a sandy substrate. Uses the lower swimming level.

Corydoras julii (Leopard Catfish, Leopard Corydoras)

Family: Callichthyidae
Length: 21/2in (60mm)
Origin: South America, lower reaches of the Amazon

Silver-grey with a pattern of black spots on the head, the middle and upper parts of the body. The dorsal fin has dark patches on the outer edge, and short barbels. Both male and female fish look very similar, with the female being slightly plumper. An egg-depositor but sometimes difficult to breed.

Requirements
Takes all foods, both live and dried, particularly worms. Water conditions are not critical 68–77°F (20–25°C). Some plants would be an advantage and a sandy substrate with pebbles and gravel. A lower level swimmer.

Hypostomus punctatus (Suckermouth Catfish)

Family: Loricardiidae
Length: 12in (300mm)
Origin: South America, Brazil

Hypostomus punctatus (Suckermouth Catfish)

The overall colouring is greenish-brown, and it is patterned all over with spots of darker colour. The Suckermouth can grow quite large but is an excellent fish for cleaning out algae from the tank. It can attack the tank vegetation if insufficient greenery is included in its diet. Not known to have bred in an aquarium.

There is confusion over the precise name of this catfish, and it can be referred to as P*lecostomus plecostomus* or H*ypostomus plecostomus*.

Requirements

Most dried and live foods taken but vegetable matter preferred. Water conditions are not critical. Temperature range 66–79°F (19–26°C). Floating plants, pebbles and small rocks necessary. Uses the lower swimming level.

Acanthopthalmus kuhli (Coolie Loach)

Loaches

Acanthopthalmus kuhli (Coolie Loach)
Family: Corbitidae
Length:41/2in (110mm)
Origin: Southeast Asia

Very shy and retiring, the Coolie Loach has a worm-like body banded with dark brown and gold patches. It loves subdued lighting and exploring through vegetation. Not known to have bred in an aquarium.

Requirements
Will take most foods, particularly worms. Water condition are not critical. Temperature about 75°F (24°C). A good selection of rocks and plants, with areas for retreat. Lower and middle level swimmer.

Botia macracanth (Clown Loach)
Family: Cobitidae
Length:51/2in (130mm)
Origin: Southeast Asia, Borneo, Sumatra

Botia macracanth (Clown Loach)

The most obvious feature of this loach is a bright orange body crossed by three vertical dark bands. Unlike other fish of this species the Clown Loach should always be kept with other fish of the same species and not on its own. No evidence of it having bred in an aquarium.

Requirements
Most live and dried foods accepted, especially worms. Water should be soft to medium-hard. Temperature between 75 and 84°F (24–29°C). Rocks, roots and some plants required with a sand and gravel substrate. Lower level swimmer.

Botia modesta (Orange-finned Loach)
Family: Cobitidae
Length:4in (100mm)
Origin: Southeast Asia, Thailand, Malaysia

A generally peaceable Loach with a grey-blue body and orange-hued fins. It has three barbels and no stripes or colour bands as many of the

Botia modesta (Orange-finned Loach)

other Loaches have. It is active at night and tends to hide away during the day. It loves digging away in the substrate. It makes clicking noises.

Requirements

Most foods taken, prefers worms and insect larvae. Water should be soft to medium-hard. Temperature around 79°F (29°C). Sand and gravel substrate required, with rocks and floating plants. Occupies the lower swimming level, hiding during daytime.

Botia sidthimunki
(Dwarf Loach, Chained Loach)

Family: Cobitidae
Length: 21/2in (60mm)
Origin: Southeast Asia, Thailand

Aptly named the Chain Loach from the patterning of the dark coloration. The overall colour is light gold with bands of dark brown on

Botia sidthimunki (Dwarf Loach, Chained Loach)

the upper part of the body. The underneath is paler. It has four barbels. It is active during the day occasionally resting on a rock or plant supported by its pelvic fins. No record of breeding in an aquarium.

Requirements

Most live and dried foods taken, but worms preferred. Water should be soft to medium-hard. Temperature range 77–86°F (25–30C). Plants, sand and pebbles required to provide retreats. Uses the lower and middle swimming levels.

Killifish

Aplocheilus dayi (Ceylon Killifish)

Family: Cyprinodontidae
Length: 21/2in (70mm)
Origin: Sri Lanka

Aplocheilus dayi (Ceylon Killifish)

A slim, elongated Toothcarp with a basic colouring of blue-grey with golden-brown on the upper flanks. Each scale is marked with a gold spot. The dorsal fin is quite far back on the body, and the anal fin is long and, in the male, pointed. It enjoys jumping and is quite active. Eggs are scattered and should be protected.

Requirements
Will accept both live and dried foods. Water should be filtered through peat if possible and should be fairly soft. Temperature range 70–77°F (21–25°C). Vegetation can be quite dense but requires swimming areas. Top level swimmer. *Note*: Fit a hood to the tank because this Killifish tends to jump.

Jordanella floridae (American Flagfish)
Family: Cyprinodontidae
Length: 2 1/2 in (65mm)
Origin: North America, Florida and Mexico

Jordanella floridae (American Flagfish)

A bulkier looking fish than other Killifish, the American Flagfish gets its name from the patterning of alternate rows of blue-green and scarlet dots over the body. These are particularly dramatic in reflected light. The caudal fin is rounded and the dorsal and anal fins have a reddish hue to them. The female, which is duller in colour, lays about 100 eggs, which the male will guard.

Requirements
Will take both dried and live foods, and also vegetable matter. Water condition is not critical. Temperature 66–74°F (19–24°C). Tank requires some plants but must have gravel substrate and rocks. Will use all levels for swimming.

Other Egg-layers

Bedotia geayi (Madagascar Rainbow)
Family: Atherinidae
Length:51/2in (140mm)
Origin: Madagascar

The overall colour of both sexes is yellowish-brown with a bright horizontal band of iridescent blue-green scales extending from the eye back to the tail. It has a short first dorsal fin and a longer second dorsal with yellow streaks. The caudal fin is pale in colour with a blue-grey outer edge. Should be kept in a shoal. Eggs are scattered among the vegetation.

Requirements
Live and dried foods accepted. Water condition is not critical. Temperature between 73 and 79°F (23–26°C). A few feathery plants should be included with gravel and rocks, but with plenty of swimming space. Swims, and feeds, in the upper levels.

Melanotaenia maccullochi (Australian Rainbow Fish)
Family: Melanotaeniidae
Length:3in (75mm)
Origin: Northern Australia

An old favourite with aquarists, the Australian Rainbow Fish is just one of a growing list of fish in this species. Overall colour is silver-blue moving to brown on the lower flanks. It has two separate dorsal fins and both dorsal and anal fins can be long and pointed. Male fins are slightly redder than on the female. Eggs are deposited or hang from plants.

Requirements
Both dried and live foods are taken. Water condition should be hard,

rather than soft, with a slight salt content (about 1 teaspoon of salt for every 8 pints/4 litres). Temperature range 71–77°F (22–25°C). Plants should be placed to allow for adequate swimming areas. Uses upper and middle swimming levels.

Opposite: Melanotaenia maccullochi (Australian Rainbow Fish)

Monodactylus argenteus (Malayan Angelfish, Mono, Fingerfish)

Family: Monodactylidae
Length:8in (200mm)
Origin: Coastal areas of the Indian Ocean from India to Australia

A silver-bodied, disc-like fish with yellow fins. The head has a dark band running vertically through the eye and a second band through the gill cover. Both dorsal and anal fins are edged with black. Both sexes are very similar. Not known to breed in aquaria.

Below: Monodactylus argenteus (Malayan Angelfish, Mono, Fingerfish)

Requirements

Will take all foods, either dried or live. The water should be hard, with about 3 teaspoons of salt added to every 21/2 gallons (10 litres) of water. Temperature 75–79°F (24–26°C). Tank should have rocks, bogwood and some plants on a gravel and sand base. Will use all swimming levels.

Tropical Live-bearers

Dermogenys pusillus (Wrestling Halfbeak)

Family: Hemirhamphidae
Length:Male 21/2in (60mm), female larger
Origins: Southeast Asia, Malaysia, Thailand, Sumatra

Dermogenys pusillus (Wrestling Halfbeak)

Elongated with long lower jaw. The caudal fin is rounded and both dorsal and anal fins are set far back on the body. Basic colouring is pale gold but greener higher up on the flanks. The male dorsal fin has red blotch. Gestation period about 8 weeks when about a dozen live young are born.

Requirements

Live foods essential. Water conditions not critical, but 1 teaspoon of salt can be added for every 11/2 gallons (5 litres). Temperature about 75°F (24°C). Dense vegetation an advantage. Swims, and feeds, in upper level.

Poecilia sphenops (Black Molly, Sphenops Molly)

Family: Poecilidae
Length:4in (100mm)
Origin: Central America

Poecilia sphenops (Black Molly, Sphenops Molly)

The male is totally black in coloration with a very large dorsal fin. Females may be black, but other paler shades are not unknown. Other hybrids are available, but the true origins of the Black Molly are vague. The female produces a brood of about 40 young.

Requirements
Will accept most foods but ensure that there is a high degree of vegetable matter. Water condition should be medium-hard and with a small amount of salt added. Temperature around 75°F (24°C). Well-planted vegetation required. Will use all swimming levels.

Right: Poecilia reticulata (Guppy, Millions Fish)

Poecilia reticulata (Guppy, Millions Fish)
Family: Poecilidae
Length:Male 1 1/2in (30mm), female up to 2in (50mm)
Origin: North coast of South America and parts of the West Indies

One of the most popular of aquarium fish. Colours vary for the different hybrids now available but, in general, the Guppy is irregularly marked in various colours. Females are duller in coloration than males, which often bear dramatically coloured tails. Guppies are ideal for the beginner. The fry should be removed from the tank.

Requirements
Most foods will be taken particularly vegetable matter. Water condition should be medium-hard. Temperature around 73°F (23°C). Plants should be fairly dense. Uses all swimming levels.

Poecilia velifera (Mexican Sailfin Molly)
Family: Poecilidae
Length:Male 6in (150mm), female 7 1/2in (185mm)
Origin: Central America, Mexico

Opposite: Poecilia velifera (Mexican Sailfin Molly)

The Mexican Sailfin Molly is very similar to the Sailfin Molly (*Poecilia latipinna*) but differs in the number of dorsal fins and the type of markings at the base of the dramatic dorsal fin. The general colouring of both sexes is pale gold with translucent blue markings. There are now many different Sailfin Mollies available. All having the same habits but varying in coloration. The female will bear upwards of 50 young.

Requirements
Will accept most foods, particularly vegetable matter. Water conditions should be hard, with 1 teaspoon of salt added to every 11/2 gallons (5 litres) of water. Temperature range 77–83°F (25–28°C). Plants required. Some form of algae essential. Will use all swimming levels.

Xiphophorus helleri (Swordtail)
Family: Poecilidae
Length:Male (excluding tail) 4in (100mm), female a little larger
Origin: Central America, Southern Mexico

The male Swordtail has an extended lower section of the caudal fin, which gives the fish its common name. The female does not have a "sword" fin. There are a number of varieties in the Swordtail family with the general colouring being from red through to orange. They are a peaceful, active species and ideal for the beginner. The female can produce anything between 50 and 100 fry.

Requirements
Most live and dried foods accepted with some vegetable matter. Water should be medium-hard. Temperature about 75°F (24°C). Plants can be quite dense but swimming areas should be allowed for. All levels used.

Xiphophorus maculatus (Platy)
Family: Poecilidae
Length:Male 11/2in (35mm), female slightly larger
Origin: Central America, Southern Mexico, Guatemala

Another of the poecilia family, which has produced many hybrids. A very popular fish which can be in almost any colour combination, from single colour to variegated multicolour. Most specimens will be of a reddish strain with patches of olive green. A female will give birth to anything between 10 and 90 young. But she should be removed to another tank for this period.

Requirements
All foods taken but should contain vegetable matter. Water conditions should be medium-hard. Temperature about 75°F (24°C). Some areas of dense vegetation required, with areas for swimming. Uses all swimming levels.

Opposite: Xiphophorus helleri (Swordtail)

Above: Xiphophorus maculatus (Platy)

Opposite: Xiphophorus veriatus (Sunset Platy, Variatus Platy)

Xiphophorus veriatus
(Sunset Platy, Variatus Platy)

Family: Poecilidae
Length:Male 21/2in (55mm), female 21/2in (70mm)
Origin: Mexico

A very good live-bearer for the beginner, but also one of which there are a number of hybrids. The general appearance is much squatter than other members of the family, usually with a body which is pale yellow or orange. The caudal fin is a darker orange and the other fins are quite pale in colour. Anything up to 150 young may be produced by the female.

Requirements
All foods taken but should contain vegetable matter. Water conditions should be medium-hard. Temperature about 75°F (24°C). Some areas of dense vegetation required, with other clearer areas for swimming. Uses all swimming levels.

Marine Tropical Fish

Tropical marine fish are a little more difficult and challenging than freshwater tropicals. The most demanding aspect being to maintain the correct water conditions and temperature necessary for the well~being of the fish. It should also be remembered that tropical marines are very often larger than freshwater tropicals

Tropical marines are some of the most beautiful and dramatically coloured aquarium fish in the world, and keeping them can be very rewarding. It is probably wiser, however, to start your aquatic experience by keeping freshwater tropicals and then move on to tropical marines when you have gained confidence and experience.

Listed below are just a few examples of Tropical Marine subjects suitable for the home aquarium.

All of the fish mentioned here require water with a 'standard mix' of synthetic seawater (kits are available from suppliers complete with instructions) which has a specific gravity of between 1.020 and 1.025 and a temperature of around 25°C (77°F)

Wrasses

Family: Labridae

Bodianus rufus Spanish Hogfish

Size: 21/2in (65mm)
Origin: Eastern Central America, Caribbean

Distinctively marked with the upper body being purple~blue and the lower part yellow. A member of the Wrasse family which is noted for

Opposite: Neon Damsel a member of the pomacentridae family, can be aggresive when it becomes an adult

its 'cleaning' action, particularly when young. Takes live foods. Sandy bottom in the tank necessary. Egg scatterer.

Opposite: Bodianus rufus Spanish Hogfish

Labroides dimidiatus
(Cleaner Wrasse, Cleanerfish)

Size: 4in (100mm)
Origin: Indian and Pacific Ocean

A prominent black stripe, widening towards the tail, on a dullish brown body. Aptly named as it 'cleans' parasites from other fish. Will take live foods in addition to its diet of parasites. Not likely to breed in the aquarium.

Left: Labroides dimidiatus (Cleaner Wrasse, Cleanerfish)

Jawfishes & Lionfishes

Opposite: Opistognathus aurifons
(Yellow~headed Jawfish)

Family: Opistognathidae

Opistognathus aurifons (Yellow~headed Jawfish)
Size: 4in (100mm)
Origin: Eastern American seaboard

A yellow head surmounting a long slender body which is silvery in colour. Makes a burrow home in the base of the tank and patrols this waiting for food. Will accept chopped meat foods. Swims in the lower levels of the tank. Unlikely to breed in the aquarium.

Pterois volitans (Lionfish)
Size: 131/2in (350mm)
Origin: Indian and Pacific Oceans

Below: Pterois volitans (Lionfish)

Reddish~brown body with very distinctive banded spikes which can be venomous for other fish and the aquarist. Voracious appetite of live foods, especially small fish. Not likely to breed in an aquarium.

Angelfish

Family: Pomacanthidae
Centropyge loriculus (Flame Angelfish)
Size: 4in (100mm)
Origin: Pacific Ocean

Centropyge loriculus (Flame Angelfish)

Orange~red body marked with five vertical dark brown stripes and a
tail which is bright yellow. Dark edges to the dorsal and anal fins. Will
take all dried and live foods and some green matter. Breeding is very
rare in an aquarium. Should not be kept with smaller fish.

Holacanthus ciliaris
(Queen Angelfish)
Length: 153/4in (400mm)
Origin: Western Atlantic

Bright yellow~green body with blue edging to dorsal and anal fins and
a yellow tail. Will take all foods, especially meat based. Swims in the
middle and lower levels. Rarely breeds in an aquarium.   **Holacanthus ciliaris (Queen Angelfish)**

Holacanthus tricolor (Rock Beauty)

Above Pomacanthus imperator (Emperor Angelfish)

Holacanthus tricolor (Rock Beauty)
Length: 231/2in (600mm)
Origin: Western Atlantic, Caribbean

Bright yellow body with a dark patch of colour covering most of the rear portion of the body from behind the gills. In young fish this patch is much smaller and it increases with age. Blue edges to the eye. Takes all foods and green matter. Not likely to breed in the aquarium.

Pomacanthus imperator (Emperor Angelfish)
Length: 131/2in (350mm)
Origin: Indian and Pacific Oceans
Young Emperors are dark blue with white stripes, often in a concentric pattern. This changes in the adult to yellow and blue horizontal

Amphiprion ocellaris (Common Clownfish)

bands. Will accept all foods, including green matter. Can be aggressive. Not likely to breed.

Anemonefish

Family: Pomacentridae

Amphiprion ocellaris (Common Clownfish)
Length: 23/4in (70mm)
Origin: Indian and Pacific Oceans

Distinctive markings of three white black~edged vertical bands on a bright orange body. All the fins carry the same white and black~banded markings. Likes to hide in sea anemones. Will accept all foods. Will deposit its eggs but breeding very rare in an aquarium.

Damselfish

Family: Pomacentridae

Abudefduf saxatilis (Sergeant Major)
Size: 63/4in (175mm)
Origin: Indian and Pacific Oceans
Blue~green body crossed by vertical darker blue bands. Should be kept with no more than three others of the species, and can be aggressive when reaching adult status. Will take all foods. Egg~depositor.

Basses

Family: Serranidae

Gramma loreto (Royal Gramma)
Size: 5in (125mm)
Origin: Caribbean

Very vivid colouring of bright violet on the head and fore part of the body. Bright yellow from the middle to the tail. Has a distinctive dark spot on the dorsal fin. Will feed on live foods, and eats plankton in the wild. Allow for retreats within rock as this is a cave~dweller. Lays eggs in a nest inside the cave, but breeding difficult.

Gramma loreto (Royal Gramma)

Surgeons & Tangs

Above: Chaetodon octofasciatus (Eight~banded Butterflyfish)

Family: Acanthuridae

Zebrasoma flavescens (Yellow Tang, Surgeon fish)

Length: 7in (180mm)
Origin: Pacific Ocean, Hawaii

Bright yellow~coloured fish with small scales, giving the fish a very smooth look. The yellow colouring covers all parts of the body except for small white marks around the base of the caudal fin. Adults and juveniles retain the same colouring. Feeds on live foods and green matter must be included in the diet. Scatterers its eggs. Comfortable in shoals.

Opposite: Zebrasoma flavescens (Yellow Tang, Surgeon fish)

Butterflyfish

Family: Chaetodontidae

Chaetodon octofasciatus
(Eight~banded Butterflyfish)

Length: 7in (180mm)
Origin: Indian and Pacific Oceans

Butterflyfish are very shy and will retreat into coral areas when they become anxious. This brightly~coloured fish has eight vertical dark bands of colour on a silvery body. The fins bright yellow and edged with black. It takes live foods and will also try to eat any sea anemones in the tank. Not likely to breed in the aquarium

Heniochus acuminatus
(Poor Man's Moorish Idol, Wimplefish)

Length: 63/4in (175mm)
Origin: Indian and Pacific Oceans, Red Sea

A very distinctive white body with two very dark bands running vertically and a very long pennant~shaped white dorsal fin. The caudal fin and the rear portion of the body are bright yellow. Takes live food, preferrably with some green matter in the diet. Does not breed in the aquarium. Swims in all levels and best kept in numbers.

Opposite: Heniochus acuminatus (Poor Man's Moorish Idol, Wimplefish)

Index

Picture Credits